In a year

Amanda Waldron

BookLeaf
Publishing

India | USA | UK

Presentation by *BookLeaf Publishing*

Web: www.bookleafpub.com

E-mail: info@bookleafpub.com

ISBN: 9789358367614

First edition 2023

To my wife of 17 years, Amy Meade, it's been a hell of a ride gorgeous. Thank you for staying. To my husband, Logan Waldron, who changed everything I ever thought of myself. Thank you for existing

Last year

This time last year I was just getting back to me. Helping my sister raise my niece. Learning how to be. Getting back to what makes me happy. back to the core of me.

I had come to terms that I was just "cool Auntie Myna" now. Little hands grasping for me, pitter patter of little feet. As the oldest child I've helped raise enough kids anyway. I needed to live for me.

It's not like I hadn't tried. But I guess I'm set in my ways. After all the nights I'd cried, wondering why I wasn't worthy of a love like mine. Why I've had the life I was born to. If I'd ever be enough...

This time last year I was just living for those around me. Fake smile firmly in place. Little did I know there was so much more waiting for me to catch up.

Last year I wouldn't have believed I'd be here today....

no such thing as "just a"

she'd always thought she was just another girl
born into a family who swept all the dirty little
secrets under the rug. if no one talks about the
horrible awful then she won't remember as she
gets older. never realizing she'd be the oldest of
three girls and would do whatever she needed to
keep them from the thoughts in her head.

she was just a black sheep compared to the
family. always outspoken. questioning everyone
and everything. curious about the most random
things. she never just accepted what she was
taught. she'd do her own research and tell you
it's all for science.

she'd always be just a woman who had been
through enough suffering. losing several friends
and beloved family members. never having luck
in love. at 30 something she just wanted peace
for the next. she knew she was meant to travel
through this life solo.

little did she know that she was days away from
meeting the one to change how she envisioned
her life. reminding her to never lose hope.

believe in the magic of wishing upon a star. the one who love her under the moon...

3

little things

it's the little things that make me happiest;
flowers growing through concrete.
or seagulls flying low over the waves.
the last rays of sunlight,
or when moonlight first hits my skin.
the radiance of a baby's smile,
or that look in his eyes when he looks at me...
you know, just the little things...

fates at the door

5

she'd had her share of knights in tin foil,
full of empty promises.
hurtful words
and the occasional bruise.

she'd done some healing
and asked some damn hard questions.
finally loving herself as a whole,
even if some days she didn't like herself.

she'd learned those lessons,
done following that pattern.
if being alone meant getting to be happy,
Then that's what she'd be.

with a gypsy heart,
and beach bum soul.
she never expected
fate was about to knock on her door.

Still not sure

When I met you I had no intention of dating
again,
finished with this thing called love.
Then there you were at my sister's,
some random guy on 420 on her couch.

What started as innocent flirting
while sharing a joint,
has become one of the most amazing
things to happen to me.

I'm still not sure why our paths crossed,
but I'm so thankful they did.
One thing I know for sure is that,
is that I belong with you n you with me...

Part of the sea

7

She'll tell you she's part mermaid when asked
about her colored hair. Most roll their eyes as
she continues on without a care

June 30, 2022

With just one look from you has me clenching
my thighs.
then you smile at me and I feel myself getting
damp.
each time you cup my jaw in your hand as we
kiss,
my heart melts a little more.
every conversation has me wanting to know
each desire.
you call yourself mine and i'm putting my faith
in that.
something was awakened the day I met you that
I hope you treat right.

surprises in the smoke

the night they met is a story to tell,
she had been in her room just hanging out.
thinking the rest of the house was out for the
count.
her mouth felt like a desert so she went to the
sink.
sees her sister standing there and does a double
take!
eyes locked with his, she asks who her friends
are..
he hops up to introduce himself offering her
some tweeds.
just a minute she replied
he didn't understand why she should change
from her t-shirt and panties.
she was intrigued by him.
and his eyes so much like hers.
this beautiful man who crossed her path,
telling about his life which sounds like the one
she's lived.
she had never felt instantly in sync with another,
not quite like this anyway.
suddenly there's a tugging at her heart
when he finally leaves.
was this another chance encounter?
or some sort of divinely timed fate?

All the things

Of all the things he could have been
He came to her chaotically beautiful.
He told her he was broken and abandoned,
A modern day outlaw on the run.

She gave him a mischievous smile
And lead him under the stars by the hand.
She told him most people have broken including
herself,
But she figured out how to make the pieces stick
back.

They lay under the stars
Talking and teasing.
By the nights end
She had a gift for him...

A slip of paper,
She said that even if they never saw the other
again;
As long as he sent word to her where the paper
said
She'd eventually find him.

Neither could believe the connection to the
other,
Almost like a fairytale.
Only he was really an outlaw,
And she simply wanted to bring peace to his life.

Eclipse

This time last year there was a different eclipse,
lunar if I remember correctly.
We barely caught that one in time,
tho we didn't have a care.

It was the beginning of Taurus season,
and both of us were Bulls.
Why was last year stepping into heaven,
& now I'm in a living hell....

if loving you is a sin

if loving you is a sin, I want to be a great sinner. if wanting you is a crime, I want to be a master criminal. if thinking about you is a curse, I want the rest of my days to be cursed. if dreaming of you is dangerous, I choose to live in danger. if leaving you is a gain, I want to be the biggest loser. if caring for you is barbaric, then call me a bargain. if living life without you is happiness, at least I have you beside me to live it with. if breathing without you is right, I want to be wrong as usual. if living with you is unholy, just remember that I've never claimed to be a saint. if spendin life with you is death, can I live & die looking in your eyes?

In alignment

She grabbed his hand pulling him behind her,
smiling like the Cheshire saying "I think you'll
appreciate this same as me".
leading them to the field to try catching the
planets align.
or was it a meteor shower only she saw as he
made her come apart for him.
she just wanted to spark some sticky green
flowers, lay under the moon and stars, maybe
discuss life and the universe, especially if he
would go with her.

One for the books

Usually if someone mentions a memorable birthday or Christmas, it's because they got the puppy or toy they really really wanted! I remember things like that as well,like the Donald duck fishing gear I think I was 6. There's also a pair of shorts and tank top from my best friend to match her when I turned 13. But I never thought I'd get a gift come close to bringing my Memaw home the day I turned 18.

Yet here he was walking into my room while I'm working to climb into bed with me. his body curling around mine, limbs getting wrapped together. he spent the day trying to see how many times he could take me over the edge, like he had radar straight to all my buttons. I spent the day on a cloud beyond 9 attempting to focus on work.

He made the day completely stress free, centered around my wishes, & the deviant desires of us both. he whispered "just one more babygirl. don't you want to come for me?" touching me everywhere. gifting me a day of complete bliss.

A new memory of another one of life's gifts that can't be bought.

where did this string come from?

I can't be for certain, but I bet my soul noticed yours within the first minutes we met. we've been searching high and low for our other half for so many years. I remember when you left that night and the further you drove away the more I felt a tug at my heart. I knew you were special the moment your eyes captured mine. just like my own, only a little more of a troubled blue. I couldn't tell you what we talked about but I remember thinking it was like I was hearing a slightly different version of my own life. knowing you also lived similar pains. once alone I lay in bed with visions of your eyes looking at me with hunger and that wolfish grin you kept giving me. just as I about fall asleep, I gently rub above my heart. a slow grin covers my face as I wonder; where did this string come from?

the idea of her

it was only 2 weeks in and you told me you love
me, I shook my head with a smile & asked "oh
yeah? Do you really or so you love the idea of
me?"

Life works out

Eventually life works itself out in ways we never imagine. I had so many big dreams growing up. To be an actress in movies. A doctor to save the ones I lost. A mother of 12! An author whose words help others not feel alone.
So many different things I wanted to be and I have been able to experience enough of life to half-assed become all those things and more. No I don't have degrees. And you should probably see a real doctor over me. Tho I've had to stitch a friend's foot because we wouldn't get to the hospital in time. I may not have any kids of my own but I'm positive I've helped raise more than 12 of them. I'm who gets called to help get others out of sticky situations because I learned how to act by reading the room.
When you have a curious mind like me, you tend to absorb as much knowledge as you can. You want to be all the things you needed when you yourself was just a child.
I've learned it's not about when life will become what you want. You gotta let go of the bullshit and become the demented hero of your own story. Start saving yourself from yourself and

trust you will end up exactly where you are
meant to. I may not know where the rest of this
life of mine is going but it brought me here.
A place I never imagined being. Here is actually
a good place to be...

Hello

21

He said he'd know me in any life because my
eyes are always the same

I never would have thought

22

A year ago today I would have laughed had I
been told I'd be married to my best friend. It's
funny how life turns out at times.
Who would have thought....